D1644690

Dear Shadows

fal

fal poetry

Olga's Dreams	Victoria Field
Keeping House	Bill Mycock

Dear Shadows

D. M. Thomas

fal

First edition 2004

copyright D. M. Thomas

All rights reserved

ISBN 0-9544980-1-1

Cover painting *Reading a Book* by Filipp Andreevich Maliavin, (Tretyakov Gallery, Moscow)

Author photograph by Valerie Josephs

Cover design by Cassie Young

Acknowledgements

Haiku Quarterly, Poetry Cornwall

Published by

Fal Publications
PO Box 74
Truro
TR1 1XS

www.falpublications.co.uk

Printed by

R. Booth Ltd
Antron Hill, Mabe,
Cornwall

To them all …

Contents

Introduction

Dear Shadows is my first new verse collection since *Dreaming in Bronze* (1981), though my Selected Poems, *The Puberty Tree* (1992), included a selection of new and unpublished verse. For the first twenty years of my writing life I wrote only verse, and dismissed any thought of writing prose fiction. My job, possibly the best in Britain – teaching nubile young women my favourite works of literature, in pleasant rooms with soft chairs and ashtrays – left me time and energy for writing poems. Then, in 1975, the College of Higher Education where I taught, which had been hectically expanding at governmental request, was listed by the same government for closure. Thereafter student numbers declined by a third each year, and colleagues found other jobs or, in the case of one close friend (the subject of the poem 'Listening to Bruckner'), committed suicide. I had too much time, and was lonelier. I suddenly felt I needed the peopled world of fiction. I started to 'make friends' – literally, in a novel.

My first published novel, *The Flute Player*, won a Gollancz/Guardian fantasy prize; my third, *The White Hotel*, became a controversial international bestseller. These were big incentives to go on writing fiction. I enjoyed creating the self-contained world that is a novel. Having decided to become a writer full-time, rather than settle for something less than the Shangri La of Hereford College, I also knew I would need to be working on projects which could absorb me for a long time, otherwise I would become bored. My fictional path was set for the next fifteen years.

My verse has always had a strong narrative element; and my novels, I felt, often followed the unpredictable path of a poem. The poem, Frost said, 'rides on its own melting, like ice on a hot stove.' I felt I didn't *really* know how to write a novel, as Iris Murdoch or Graham Greene would write it; and I was forgetting how to write poems. I no longer knew quite what I was. My confusion deepened when, in 1995, I accepted an invitation to write a biography of Alexander Solzhenitsyn. Writing a factual, scholarly book felt totally alien – even though I tried to write it in a novelistic way. I don't regret writing it; I regarded it, alongside my translations of Pushkin and Akhmatova, as my small tribute to Russian literature, which has given me so much. But those three years exhausted me.

During that period, my late wife Denise was found to have incurable cancer. It was a very painful time. When the biography was out of the way, I found some solace in looking through the tattered photograph albums which my family had filled with their snapshots. My father came home from California in 1929 with a much-loved, long, brown camera, which served him well right up to the era of colour. I started to write plain free verse poems about the snaps. Pasternak writes in *Doctor Zhivago* that 'art is always meditating upon death, and thereby always creating new life.' In the midst of sickness, grief and despair I found some 'new life' in seeing father and mother, aunts and uncles, in the aliveness of the moment when a picture was taken. These poems and snapshots make up the first section of this book.

Writing poems again has been hard – even harder than it used to be. It's like picking up a tennis racket after a ten or twenty year lay-off. The slashing forehand drives that used to zing effortlessly across the net – at least some of the time – now just dribbled into the net or flew off the racket-rim. You have to practise afresh what used to come naturally. One help in this process has been the poem with strict form, such as the sestina and the sonnet. It may seem strange that a strict form, which ought to make the poetic process harder, actually makes it easier; but the strict rules act as a kind of cliff-climb hand-rail. One of the set forms I've tried is the *rondeau redoublé*, in which certain lines have to be repeated, at different points in the poem, and there are only two rhymes. Trying to describe in this form my feelings when shopping in Tesco's on a Sunday morning, and recalling my chapel-going youth, proved almost impossibly demanding. I probably have two or three hundred drafts, written over a year. But it was fun! After the laboriousness of a 250,000 word biography, it felt wonderfully releasing to be again able to insert a comma in the morning, and take it out in the afternoon.

In turning again to verse I have also returned to the landscape in which I am rooted, Cornwall. Along with the poems, I've written my first play, set in Cornwall: *Hell Fire Corner*. It is due its first performance at the Hall for Cornwall in Spring 2004. The verse collection and the play are emotionally closely related.

And where now? More poems? A novel? I've no idea. It's autumn; the air is bracing. Pushkin, in the last stanza of his poem 'Autumn', describes his creative mood as resembling that of mariners hoisting the sails on a ship; and he ends: 'We sail. Where shall we sail …'.

D.M.Thomas
October 2003
Truro, Cornwall

Note

In the first section, *Snapshots*, the lives of my parents' generation and earlier, glimpsed through old photos, are interpreted by my fallible memory and knowledge. It would have been untruthful to memory to have corrected factual inaccuracies if they came to light (a few did), and I have not done so.

The photograph on p29 is by David Hills.

1

Snapshots

The Founding

Where I was born. The next house to the right;
thirty years beyond this frozen moment
of the chapel's founding in warm evening sunlight.
I don't exist yet, but these are my people,
and this my village, founded on tin and copper.

Such a grand chapel, built by their own hands
and faith. That tide whipped up by Wesley
still hasn't ebbed. The mines still haven't closed.
I think it's my grandfather William
at the back, the left-side portal,
near a woman with an extraordinary tilted hat:
it's his hair receding, his droopy moustache,
his attitude slightly distanced, as befits
a one-quarter Italian, if the legend's true.
It makes sense, too, that he came out from the service
last, being the organist.
Everyone loves the pews he's carved.

I guess my grandmother and their older children
are here somewhere. Sometimes I glimpse my favourite
aunt's, Cecie's, craning, anxious face. My father
and mother, in their cots no doubt, a few hundred yards
apart, are probably sleeping.
What are they dreaming at this very moment?
Is it somewhere recorded?

Truth for all these is as firm and strong
as their summer shadows, as the corsets
the women feel content to be wearing,
shaping them for their best dresses.
They don't envy or resent their menfolk
slaving down the mines, dying young
of silicosis or phthisis or accidents.
Haven't heard of sexual politics,
but feel, life is a struggle
and we're all, we working folk, in it together.

Even if they knew something called a
Theory of Relativity was published
a few days ago, and could understand it,
they wouldn't give a fig. They only know
there is a Promised Land,
this was some handsome day, the singing
was handsome, and they're so lucky
to be living in modern times when
a man can come up from Redruth and click away,
so they can geek at themselves and say
'Look at Evie, you –some hat that was!'
and shriek with laughter till they almost wet themselves.

July 6 1905

In Love with Time

They were in love with time, and with each other,
These people from whom I come – and so forever
Were taking pictures, conveying to their future
Moments of their being: themselves,
As though they were egotists and not
The humble, gentle people that they were;
As if they were Kennedys they posed together:
Brothers and sisters, spouses, neighbours, friends,
The closeness of a working-class Cornish village
Transposed at times to California, Melbourne,
Yet taking the family and the village with them,
Capturing themselves in thousands of small snapshots
That spill, from cardboard-boxes, falling-apart
Brown albums, a snowstorm of images.

The people now all dead, save I and my sister;
And when we die, the photos will die truly;
No one, then, to say, She ran a sweet-shop,
He worked at Clotworthy's outfitters, she
Lost husband, both daughters and a grandchild
To tuberculosis, and possibly had an affair
With a mine-captain – my saddest aunt – and he
Was engineer in a silver-mine in Colombia
Then retired to Muswell Hill and a sickly wife...
They'll be lost in the inevitable blur
Who were in love with time, and with each other.

And already I say, I don't remember who they were...

Snapshots

1

I don't know who they are –
my mother, my father,
a few days after their wedding.
Silent the creak and motionless the pitch
of the S.S.'Berengaria', heading for New York.
He has come home for her, his village girl.
Ignorant of the very word ballet, she is Anna Pavlova
swooning in his strong arms,
and he, whose only poems are the hymns
in the Methodist hymnbook, is triumphant Mayakovsky
with his mistress Lili Brik, set to conquer the New World.
They glow in their love-trance; even Leslie,
his kid brother, whom they're taking with them
to the El Dorado, doesn't get a look in;
while the rest, extras, Cornishmen and one faded wife
seeking work, have no identities
and no future. Just these two.

Holding her, he has glimpsed at last
the soft white body; no more than that yet:
she is seasick; and will be, till the last day
of the voyage. He will never truly penetrate,
to his life's end, her winter greatcoat.
Though they'll go on singing love-songs, each to each.

1923

2

The two on the right are out of reach:
the plain one, and the signora with red lips;
mother and daughter maybe; they recur.
I'm four or thereabouts. Grey battleships
are nosing out of Chatham, Devonport,
and D-Day troops, in time, will throng this beach;
but today the light, the air's transparency,
glows on my father's white and creaseless shirt,
and my laughter, leaning on him, is utterly pure
and radiant with unshadowed joy.
My sister's pop is cold, and hot the tea,
and they will stay so, beyond entropy.

circa 1939

3

Entre deux guerres, two of these uncles and aunts,
standing behind their aged parents in the small front garden,
I never met – the two in bow-ties.
Percy, the oldest, will go off to California,
marry fat Luella, and return for a holiday
at eighty, unfortunately to a house
listing from too many deaths, and poised to sink.
I didn't meet him. Couldn't face the wreck.

The other, Donald, the youngest. He doesn't know,
with his shy smile, he'll die very soon,
a trainee airman, crashing on Salisbury Plain.
His death will destroy my grandmother,
already frail-looking, and bring, to comfort her,
my father and Leslie and their wives
home from America. I was given his name.
A laughing charmer, they said, a devil for the girls,
and had a rich singing voice. He doesn't know,
gazing into the lens, aiming for flying and fucking
and singing, this is almost as far as it goes.

A moment later, they move, they move about
on the daisied grass,
and Donald cracks a joke.

c.1923

4

I remember that overcoat,
ill-fitting, worn until it was threadbare
and he was dead; and that hunched,
infinitely defeated look.
What quelled him, hammered him into the ground?
Not simply the backbreaking work, day in day out,
not simply the desperately craving libido,
not simply the unfulfilled intelligence:
was it that he had touched gold too early,
and never found it again?

I don't know,
but something unsatisfied in him
runs through me like sand through an hourglass,
like sand through a mesh.

During the 'smash-and-grab raid' on his prostate,
his oppression will briefly lift
– he will ask only to 'sing again, and see the fields,
and be with you, Amy' –
between the complication and the blood-clot.

c. 1957

5

It was painful to keep my eyes open
while my Daddy was fumbling with the camera
and I wished he'd hurry up,
outside Mona's cottage at Restronguet,
the tin hat on my head, toy gun on my shoulder:

not memory but living experience,
the thoughts I had then
still here! the snapshot a trigger for
the moment itself! feeling proud
of being a soldier...

the sunlight too bright, my daddy too slow:
in the blinding brightness, through dappled leaves
above the creek, my eyes closing
as the camera clicks.
The sun's simply too heavy.

c.1940

6

I'm more conscious of the complications
of that terra australis under their smooth dresses
than they are: I know the tensioned coolness
between roll-on and nylons under
her sedate skirt better than Lois,
who'll gratefully, as a young widow, turn to trousers
and pop-socks. No real girls around, I love to
play hookey from school, peel off my hot doublebreasted
grey suit and explore the exquisite mixture
of fear and excitement, constriction and freedom.

Equally I know the heavy comfort
of my mother's pink boned sidehooked corset
beneath silk bloomers she wears
throughout our time in hot Australia. They'll help me
to beat all the Jewish boys
in my fourth year exams. A talisman,
that motherly silk around my groin
as I parse Latin verbs.

They know me as the Billy Bunter
who's got fat from the suety fish-and-chips –
an English consolation for my homesickness –
Mum brings home to me each afternoon
on the way from the stocking factory.
I'm at an awkward age anyway, and they'll chuckle
at the way I've poked my tongue out
at my brother-in-law. They don't know
how confused I am between the two matronly women,
how they blend into a single unattainable girl.

1950

7

This picture the foundation-stone
of the dynasty of snapshots – circa 1870 - 1960.
My father's paternal grandparents.
Great-grandfather William stands confused,
arms hanging apelike: great-grandmother's
face is sour under the lacy white cap.
Not a close marriage, one guesses.
I only know he drank away the family pub,
and she was one of twins, half-Italian;
her father an itinerant artist, some minor
Michelangelo, one of many brought to paint
the high ceiling at Tehidy Manor; – or –
less romantically – a silversmith,
i.e. pawnbroker. Anyway,
he fled back to Italy, and his Cornish wife
'never smiled again'. She taught her daughter,
with her Sicilian Mafia face and crouch, the same trick.
Her hair's still black; and I imagine it raven
and long and flowing, the locks of a Mona Lisa,
the ruby lips uptilted, provoking; and her eyes...

But soused William, all his married life,
has been shadowed by her lost father,
that improvisatore – who came to paint a ceiling,
got a Methodist girl into trouble,
brought to a family of miners, publicans, farmers
and carpenters an occasional dark Mediterranean look
varying the redheaded Celt, and possibly
the wayward artistic gene – before he fucked off
from responsibility and the chill rains,
back to his own tongue, radiant skies, olive-breasted girls.
Ciao, great-great-grandad!

c. 1870

8

Everything's still novel in LA! Walter Pigeon,
the film star, has even dandled cute little
Lois on his lap, in a break from movie making
at Twentieth Century Fox. Dad's only a workman there,
but this is the land of democracy, and everyone's
respected. In truth the young Cornish couple
are handsome enough to be starring themselves! The sun
embraces them with unfadable light and warmth.
There's so much twenties gaiety the ladies could all
kick their legs up in a Buzby Berkeley chorus.
I guess Leslie holds the Kodak. His Cornish bride,
like a tall gawky deb who can't believe her luck,
is in the line, and Lilie, Dad's sister.
Donald, the kid-brother, might be here too,
but he's chosen to join the Royal Air Force,
and his mother's anxious – though thanking the dear Lord
it's peacetime. The endless snaps are for her.
Later, the clan will climb laughing aboard Dad's Model-T,
heading back to the neat, white, Hispanic house
they're renting dirt-cheap
on Beverly Hills. Dorothy Parker's down the street.

c.1926

9

In the field behind 'Beverly',
the tiny bungalow he's built after-work,
two miles from the family home nestling under
Carn Brea just above my head,
he is teaching me – not rugby,
which he has never played – but pride:
in our team, our race,
our class.
            How, for example,
Bert Solomon, in the Edwardian twilight,
climbed up the interminable ladders
of Crofty, saw to his carrier pigeons,
which were more to him than rugby,
took the Friday night milk-train
to London, then with his mercurial grace
phantomed through the Welsh
to win the match for England; left the toffs
– public school, Oxbridge – panting far behind,
gaping. But at the celebration dinner
was all thumbs, graceless with the cutlery
and grammar. Went home by the milk-train
to his pigeons, the crippling
tin-mine, and refused
to play for England again.
Yet he'd done enough, had shown
that not all the lilies of the field,
who toiled not, neither span,
could match the Cornish working-man,
Solomon in all his glory.

c.1939

10

Cecie's life seems altogether carnal –
it's she who feeds the chickens and chops off their heads,
mangles the baskets of steaming laundry,
mows the lawn, empties chamber pots,
looks after my motherless cousin, Gerald;
she's the stay-at-home, the willing skivvy,
absorbed in the terraced row which is Carnkie,
its brambled lanes amid the minestacks,
sunk between two carns... Carnal, and without romance,
her whole huge capacity for love
invested only in the family. The Great War
has scythed through the lads. But this one snap
hints of a dream that won't be fulfilled.
God knows who he is, or what happens to him.
I like to think they made love in Carn Brea's bracken
– mother's boy though he looks, I hope her
highly-sexed nature knows the throbbing bliss
as his portly stomach moves upon her:
something to put beside her father's fumbles
in the vestry after his organ-playing; and
giggly tickles with Nellie in their sad bed.

c.1920?

11

But – to compare sadnesses –
Cecie's bondage to the family house and
Nellie's eternal engagement to a dead soldier
can't compare with their eldest sister's. Ethel's
face is thoughtful even before TB,
the Yezhovshchina of the poor in cold,
damp cottages, has skilfully erased
like a Stalinist censor her two beautiful
daughters (not to mention a still-unborn granddaughter).
Her husband too – a miner
she only ever referred to by his surname: Kendell.

And what of (as legend has it) her lover, a mine-captain?
Is that affair over? Did Kendell or conscience
draw her back? Is he paying her out with blows
or, with the inflamed eros of TB,
a frenzy of sex? Will she blame her great sin
for the holocaust? No wonder she'll always
seem cheerless, at least till a late second marriage –
too sad to be likeable.

c.1925

12

In a lost photo she's like
an amalgam of her two gorgeous daughters;
and even here – I think my father must have said
something droll – there is, for once, a charming
and only half-suppressed smile, making us glimpse
what her lover had seen in her. But those girls!
How could 'consumption' have carried off,
within a year or two, that sumptuous and
voluptuous Italianate figure on the right?
At the other end, my mother's holding the arm of
her father, looking like a half-sozzled Kerry farmer.
Everyone here's so sharply within their life
death can't for a moment hold a candle to it.

c.1930

13

My father would like to hold time still,
always seeming to gaze, thoughtfully,
in the opposite direction from everyone else.
He'd like to keep this garden that he loves
as it is; he'd like to bring back his sister
Ethel's beautiful girls. You can see
she just wants to die, to get back to them.

I don't know who the girl is, on the grass by Lois.
I like the strong, graceful poise
of Elsie, Eddie's wife, her arms stretched
to cup her knee as she leans forward
to make more room. The lazy summer day,
that makes Cecie's eyes heavy, and gives Nellie
a look of radiant health and attractiveness,
is so potent still, amid the shimmer of tiny leaves,
my gaze travels up
the taut sheen of Elsie's lisle stockings
to where they go out of sight and into mind:
as she herself will soon, for these others,
and for Eddie and their small child. TB again.

c.1933

14

So far from home, the American boys
are always welcome: a meal from Mum,
and from Dad a gentle warning that
Lois is only eighteen. And welcomed by
the larger family on Sundays.

          I've always thought
this one was Jimmy; yet when
my sister – her hand, at seventy, still flying
to her locket – says with horror, 'No,
that's not Jimmy! I don't know who
he is', I too remember Jimmy
as different, solider, craggier; and it can't
be pre-D Day, as it would have to be –
it would make my gangling cousin Gerald,
towering over his father, an impossible thirteen.
Who knows, then, who he is, and why he's here?

But I can recognise
The Sunday kindness, handed out to Jimmy;
the chapel in the background he'll
be ushered towards at five to six,
after the canned peaches he's provided.
Jimmy, from Texas, lavishes gifts:
nylons, gum and whole cartons of
Lucky Strikes; yet probably, at twenty-seven,
is too old and – who knows? –
experienced for Lois. So best to

surround him with genteel family happiness,
ageing spinsters, a widower, two watchful schoolboys,
where no one (not even, or rarely, my father)
is having sex. And praise the babyfaced
Australian, somewhere in the Middle East, she's kind of
engaged to, while passionately in love with Jimmy.

?

15

She's engaged to him, but
will Harold really come back for her
from Los Angeles? So much glamour there,
so many dressy, educated girls...
All she can do is look sideways at him from under
her mop of frizzy black hair, and hope
her bright eyes still have the same appeal,
and her lips... But it's so far; going to work
on winter mornings, or coming home at night,
walking those six miles from the fuse factory,
she knows sadly he doesn't even see the same stars.

c.1922

16

The stars are home from Hollywood,
and stun the village with a car!
not bad for a young working-man,
with his beautiful wife dolled-up
like Mary Pickford, and the latest camera!
The unmarried girls are proud of their brother
and charmed by the American-speaking little girl,
but grandpa and grandma are sombre,
thinking of the son who won't be coming back.
But at least grandma can get a lift to the churchyard,
where, every day, she sighs, and thinks, This
is where I'm comfortable, here with my precious...
'Now you sit here, Harold,' says Cecie,
and Amy takes the Kodak. And the villagers think,
'Look at they, you! some grand they are!'...

c.1929

17

The groom has packed, for their honeymoon in Bournemouth,
a packet of condoms, Bishop Butler's
Analogy of Religion and Bertrand Russell's History
of Western Philosophy. In fact, Lois will chuckle,
he won't open any of them (the books);
but he's a serious young man, and dazed
from a sense of enormity. It was a long
voyage for a girl he dated for only a week
when the aerodrome was mist-shrouded. Navigating
on bombing-raids was less frightening
than this, and Leslie had to lean forward in his pew
to murmur gruffly 'Ray!' as he seemed
about to faint. Lois too is dazed;
she loves him, but she'd forgotten how short
he is, especially compared with Jimmy, and wishes
he were still in his dashing RAAF uniform.

          Ray will die,
in his fifties, a heart-attack victim
like his father, and have his funeral in
the garden he'll be so proud of
in their nice suburban home. His son, Lloyd, will come
to Britain as a ballet-dancer, and live with
(he'd turn in his grave) a ballerina from Rome,
so repeating, in a sense, our family's Italian connection.

Everything's in motion, that looks so solid;
Bishop Butler's religion's about to collapse,
western thought is primed to assimilate living in sin,
homosexuality, easy divorce, abortion, Ray's daughter

will choose to give birth without a husband,
agony aunts who have helped keep Lois pure
will be encouraging masturbation and responsible
premarital sex – everything looks just-so,
the white gloves, gay hats, buttonholes,
but it's turning and turning like the great globe.

1947

18

From the Globe Inn, which my great-grandfather
drank away – the dark building nestling
over the shoulder of a ruined engine-house –
to the Wesleyan chapel that generations of us
helped to build, played the organ or sang in –
just out of sight above the whitewashed shape of
'St.Martin's Villa' – Carnkie is in terminal coma.
As the old folk die off,
they're replaced only by some overspill
pensioner couples from up-country, in bungalows
facing the old mining-terrace and thereby
blotting out the green fields
rising to Basset Carn. The newcomers
know nothing of religious passion, or the other
aspects of Cornish tribalism, but tend
their little gardens and watch the telly.

The new owners of 'St.Martin's' – kindly
friends – have built a garage and sheds
on the sweet-scented lawn with its long garden seat,
framed by shrubbery, which seemed timeless,
the scene of fifty years of snapshots.
Soon, a family of tinkers
will buy the fadedly elegant old house,
given to us a century ago by a mine-captain
who lacked children to inherit it. Our drawing-room
which echoed with 'Nirvana', 'Wanting You' and
'Pale hands I loved Beside the Shalimar', the tinkers

will fill with piles of tyres and engine parts.
No wonder I'm scowling in this photo, though
there's also a touch of the poet's arrogant pose.

c.1968

19

They can afford to strut a bit, and pose –
in the city of Clark Gable, Douglas Fairbanks.
Smart dressers, earning good money,
singing in a church choir... My father,
later, will forget his confident strut.
Leslie writes on the back of the snap:
We are looking towards the mountains. The city
is right at our back.' Frames in his mind
an image of Lois, his fiancée, soon to join them.
My mother, wondering when she'll be pregnant
but in no great hurry, rather likes the name Lois,
if it's a girl. They're all three at the peak,
head-high with the mountains, in the prime,
as young as the confident century
and they've already struck gold.

c.1924

20

It's all a jolly romp on the Marigold
coach, the Sunday School Outing, but really
the village's birthday, because we're all
one family: Iris Prisk, Mrs Adams, Mrs Waters, May Kemp,
Marie Richards, Phyllis Webb, Percy Kemp the organist,
his clever daughter Valerie, Rosemary Waters,
who in the shrieking coach as we head up the Goss Moor
will tell me not to turn round as she's doing
'running repairs', her dress hoisted; and Mrs Adams'
heavy cake and Mrs Waters' saffron
will be passed around and sampled, and my mother,
who's not a keen cook, will contribute
one of those nice sponges from Mrs Webb's shop.

c.1952

21

The sun is here now, enchanting,
a peculiar radiance, perhaps only
for a few seconds, perhaps for a whole
Sunday afternoon: a beauty magnified
by the uncut grass, the multitude
of daisies and marigolds. The sky's a heavenly blue
over Carn Brea, in front of them, the chapel
– to which later they will go to worship –
to their left. Cecie's shadow
suggests it's about three. There's no shadow
cast by the concrete garage and shed
that will destroy this haven
forty years from now. All this
is eternal; an emanation of the
'love that will not let me go'
they sang in the morning service,
Donald's fine voice reminding poignantly
of the absent boys.

On the back someone has written: 'June 10th 1926. TAKEN
IN OUR GARDEN Left to right: Cecie, Lois, Mr Cox,
        Nellie & Mrs Cox.'
Mr and Mrs Cox are mysterious presences
in several photos; summer visitors
from upcountry; I know nothing of them.
Lois is dreaming of her fiancé in Los Angeles

and waiting for a berth. Cecie and Nellie
have grown into their spinsterhood; the cat
is happy for the moment to be still.
There's no oppressiveness, the air is fresh;
the faint, delightful breeze from the sea
will never vanish, nor the shrubs be tossed
by a raging wind. This is the word everlasting.

1926

22

I dream that there's a website for the dead,
and they can all – including my mother's brother
Stevie, weak from miners' silicosis,
and his wife Susan-Jane, who's pleasant
and kindly, I remember, and who will
do something utterly dramatic
after Stevie's death: stand naked
outside Carnkie Methodist chapel, her words
lost in the wind and drizzle – can all
communicate again, telling their story,
gossiping, creating a novel,
as living as they are here.

c.1953

23

A moment after the Kodak clicks,
it is likely that Tommy Gunn,
Lilie's husband, will raise one buttock
with a sudden stillness of expectancy
like the brief silence after a lightning flash,
then unloose a loud, theatrical fart.
Luella's little girl, giggling,
will bury her head in her mother's
capacious lap; Lilie will flush
almost as red as her hair and
rebuke him gently: 'Tommy!'
No one can understand why such a genteel woman
married so crude a man.
My father's faraway look will be startled away.
Cecie, in far-off Carnkie, always says,
'Wherever you may be, let your wind
and your water run free...' herself
a natural, though unhistrionic, farter.
Tommy will live to a ripe old age,
Lilie will die of stomach cancer after the war.

c.1926

24

He's waging war for the Foreign Legion.
'The Desert Song'. Redruth Amateur Operatic.
It's the only society he'll ever join,
except for chapel choirs and the union.
When they write his funeral notice in the 'West Briton'
I'll be angry they can find so little
to say about him – who was, for me, the world.
He's rehearsed his one line in the operetta
over and over at home:
'You can't come in, Emile, you're drunk.'
He's not a convincing sentry;
I can't imagine him thrusting his bayonet through a Riff
or a German – though he was in the Home Guard,
and said he'd follow his officer anywhere.
He's not, though, the confident man of California,
something has changed him, there ought to be
a Foreign Legion for the meek, the gentle,
somewhere they can begin over.
But he sings, at home, with Amy,
'Only a Rose' so wonderfully,
you know he's not in our small living-room at all,
and you see him, in a red cloak,
serenading his love by the shadowy campfire.

c.1948

25

Resolutely they decline to
smile at one another, or at the camera,
or even acknowledge the other's presence,
even though it's (I'm guessing) their golden
anniversary. He is waiting to return to
his harmonium in the drawing-room. When he worked
in the mine he loved his craft so much
he'd run to his carpenter's bench; but now
his sons joke, 'Father's heard a voice say,
work no more!' Eliza is still brooding on
Donald; though Billy too wears a black tie
three years on. He just
doesn't speak of his grief. She remembers
when he was due home from Johannesburg
but got embroiled on the ship with a hussy.
All the deaths loom large: the first William,
the first Nellie, who lived only a few months.
There's something quite heroic about
their refusal of hypocrisy, in front of
the celebration cake, the bottle of Port.

1931

26

Lois and our favourite uncle, Eddie,
striding out down the road from Peace
to Carnkie. She's brought her three-year-old daughter
to England for a trip, Ray's gift to her.
The eight-month stay is flying by. I see
little of her – in the Army, learning Russian.
Dad's face – she'll tell me in after-years--will crumple
as her train draws out. They'll never meet again,
and never discuss certain memories. Unromantic Ray
will greet her joyfully with a record:
'Je t'aime'. Lois's mind will be full of a shipboard romance
with a White Russian en route for Sydney and a bride.
Naïvely perhaps she'll confess it – a little dancing,
a few kisses, are surely forgivable amid the stress
of looking after a toddler on a monthlong voyage?
But Ray will turn cold, and to praying
at odd times. The marriage will never be quite
the same again; and not till
almost his last heart attack will she tell him
why she could never stand having her breasts touched
and so on.
But right now she's happy,
having a giggle with Eddie, bouncing homealong;
the fresh wind from the north cliffs aiding their stride.
This is where she belongs. Unknown to her still
the charming face in the phosphorus glow of
the Indian Ocean, beside her at the rail, and Ray's
Je t'aime. It was around this spot too that I,
a few years earlier, after an agonisingly shy
walk with my first 'date' around the Carn,
drew her into the hedge and – speaking almost for
the first time – murmured huskily, 'Baissez-moi!'
And wondered why she declined to see me again.

1955

27

I can't see that schoolboy
pretending to be interested in throwing snowballs
as in any way different from
almost every other figure in the albums,
who are dead. Even though
I recall so well the almost unique
snowfall and bitter cold, and even
this moment itself, picking up the handful
of snow and looking at the camera –
I don't really see him as closer
to me, my breathing self, than say my father, my mother,
Percy Kemp at the chapel organ.
In fact, for all, the words dead and alive,
Or self and other, seem peculiarly irrelevant –
or they co-exist, in a stark beauty,
like the extreme whiteness and blackness here
beneath our kitchen window where the Cornish range
is ablaze and my mother
is making stew for Harold when he comes
exhausted and freezing home from work,
laying block after block after block.

1947

28

In the last of the century of snapshots,
an elfin girl amid Ireland's rocks and water.
Making love
in a fifteen-bob a night guest-house
in Sligo, looked down on
by a picture of Jesus with a bleeding heart,
and several crucifixes.

Our first, stolen holiday.
And now I pray to that Jesus in pain
for life everlasting,
for life everlasting.

1966

2

Coitus Interruptus

Night

Of all the nights we spent together
the one I cherish most
was a few months before you died
when you were far too sick for any passion
and even to be held was painful.

Normally, heroically thoughtful,
you did not wake me in the night to share
your pain and terror;
but that night you whispered, 'Are you awake?'

We lay and talked, our hands clasping
across the bed we'd had to order,
wide, wide, both chary of touches.
Tears choked in my throat
thinking of that huge, unimaginable
amputation of so great a part of
myself from myself, yet knowing that
it would not be total, as it would be
for you. You asked me
did I believe in life after death.
I said I believed time an illusion.

Our hands staying clasped, we drifted
into silence. At some point you fell asleep
and still we were together;
and at some point, later, I too slept,
and still we were together.

Language

This is the dying ward. She finds it hateful.
She has been here before, three months ago,
When she could still walk. She was met by Gay,
Who told her, 'We're the well ones at this end.'
She saw Gay driven off by her husband
To buy a new kitchen at Asda;
Only her dead eyes were a giveaway.
But no one expected, when she went home on Friday,
She'd be back on Monday, comatose;
And Denise watched her die, across from her, slowly,
While her husband and son pretended to watch
Wimbledon on the big screen near her bed.

That was Denise's educational visit:
To teach her how to use stencils,
But really that dying isn't frightening.
And neither worked. Too ill for the first,
Not ill enough for the second.

So now she's back, she knows for the last time,
And she hates this ward where only she
Has any spirit still.
They wheel her bed to the tiny smoking-room
At the other end, and she spends the day there,
Till they bring her back early to be changed.

The nurse says, taking a pillow away,
'Now settle down, dear, and try to sleep.'
The nurse crosses to a half-comatose patient.
'What a fucking place, where I can't even have
A fucking cigarette!'
'Language!' cries the nurse, scurrying across.
'There's no need for bad language!'
'It wasn't personal,' Denise says.

In the end they wheel her to the smoking-room
Away from the other patients
Who know what a fine place the hospice is;
Are quietly grateful,
And have no need for language.

A Short History

Screwing my students seemed as natural
As reading Yeats to them; I loved the hunt.
My colleague's babysitter was too slender,
Nervy, flat-chested, but I thought she had spirit
In those green eyes, as she tipped a balloon
From my tipsy leap, my smiling wife at my side.

Sec. Mod. her origin, and one could hear it
In her sharp Cockney wit, her put-downs blunt;
But my marriage, rumour told her, had all but died.
She babysat for us; then, parked, the swell
Of a soft thigh, stress of a black suspender,
Before she said, ' You want too much, too soon'--

Moving my hand away. I liked 'too soon',
She, that I took denial in good spirit,
Showing respect. And soon, indeed, I went
Where she taught Yeats's gyres from the inside,
Seductive, tense and unpredictable.
In lay-bys I was Leda, brushed by splendour.

She left. College was done, and I was tied
To wife and kids. But we couldn't break the spell;
She brought life back to me, the Holy Spirit.
We held firm, like the stockings and suspenders
She wore against the trend of tights and Quant,
Loving their play of contrasts, like the moon.

As the years passed, I'd wonder if my tides
Moved solely to her dark, magical cunt,
The long droughts worth it for the short monsoons.
We'd fall so easily from heaven to hell,
When angers made it hard to find the spirit.
We fucked, or fought, or both, with no surrender.

Generous, awkward, disaster-prone, unquell-
able; abrupt at times with adults, tender
To pets and the small children she would guide
To a sense of what art, nature, reading meant.
Gentle and shy yet – lover of fags and spirits
And shocking the prissy – loud as a bassoon.

A painful labour couldn't quench her spirit:
'God, what a job – staring up women's cunts!'
She told a startled doctor. We had tied
A loose, half-secret knot; and then as soon
As Ross was born – divorce: so casual
It slipped loose like a careless, rushed suspender,

And we stayed married, both in law and spirit,
Unknowingly. She'd one affair that went
Deeper than my brief flings. Our next son died
Before his birth. My little grandson fell
Into our swimming pool. Then, all too soon,
She found it painful, flexing her neck to tend her

Beloved flowerbeds. Physio didn't clear it.
I was with her when consultants hummed and lied.
Joked to a surgeon, at her pre-med, 'Well,
It will be harder to find men who want
An iron cage than stockings and suspenders!'
Floated off then, like that first blue balloon;

And even with a harness to suspend her
Over a bath, kept up a joking front.
I found, surprised, our love had been all spirit;
And on a night of an amazing moon
I said to her, 'Denise, all shall be well;
God loves you.' Her eyes opened, and she died.

Love Letters

Creative, well-read, something stopped her writing.
Perhaps her mother, critical and tart.
In the same way, she didn't wear her heart
Upon her sleeve. So I'd nothing in her hand
Save for some shaky things-to-bring I'd find
Scrunched in my pocket – scraps of envelope:
'cigs, check pyjamas...' 'knickers, 3 clean nighties,
chocs...' (for the nurses). 'Flannel, cigs, bar soap...'
I'd feed on these few remnants of Denise
Like passionate letters sent by Heloïse

To Abelard. Today, a treasure-trove –
Some phrases in a notebook: questions for
The hospice doctors, barely legible;
Then something that is almost about our love:
Our house's silence, how I would rarely smile,
Though now 'Don is v.g.' And I rejoice,
Even as the tears spring to my eyes once more,
Hearing again her dry, beloved voice.

Rubbing Against You

Browsing an old softporn magazine
that came to light in a garage drawer,
I start to read an unusually literate
'intimate confession'; at last recognising
the anonymous interviewer
is me: I'm electrified to read words
you spoke to me two decades ago,
in your flat, in bed, smoking,
earning us some money
that would take us part-way to Venice.

Your erotic adventure with the young teacher
I remember: how you undressed each other
one night during a school trip
when your pupils were safely in bed;
how he felt he was floating;

but I didn't remember
how you weren't averse to a bit of frottage,
when you were hot... the rather attractive man
pressed up against you in the bus,
pretending to read his paper
but really rubbing himself against you.
How you 'pretended to sway with the bus',
but were 'really playing up to him.
I must have been really hot
because I had an orgasm.'

Unquenchable desire and torment
as I frot against my fingers.
I want to ask more questions:
'Did he know you were aware of him frotting?'
'Did he come, as he read his paper?'
'Do you think he knew you orgasmed?'
Even dead, you turn me on like crazy. I'm
that man, stepping dazed from the bus,
walking on air, my crotch soaked and not caring.

Dream Scenes

1

You've been away
or I've been away
for several months and
I've come to pick you up; the restaurant
where we decide to have a meal
seems to be closing, the lights are
being dimmed, except for our corner where
they push two tables together as if
to fit other people in. And indeed
another man joins us, sitting opposite you,
and you obviously have spent time together, you're
conversing with him rather than me
and I get the sick, excited feeling
you and he – smoothly goodlooking, called Max –
have been intimate during our separation.

You flit off, to the toilets,
and he does too, leaving me alone,
trying to peer at the limited menu
almost unreadable under the still-dimming light.
Worried about you and him
I clatter down two flights of stairs
to look for the loos; but then I hear you
from the top of the stairs calling, 'Don!'
and you come down to me and say,
'You must be kind to him, he's not well.'

Your hair, still jet-black at your death,
straight and short, has suddenly become grey
and in an elderly perm; you're fat-bellied and
in a shapeless frock; you say, 'Sometimes
I hardly think it's worth getting up in the mornings;
I've let myself go.' 'Yes, you have!' I reply,
knowing how you hoped
I'd disagree with you whenever you made
a self-disparaging remark about your appearance,
and wanting to punish you, hurt you,
for letting yourself go,
letting yourself go.

2

You pursue me through a giant, empty hospital
with murder in your eyes.
Terrified, at full stretch, I weave
in and out of wards and corridors,
but although you're hobbling, crippled,
and have to stop often
to go into a toilet to be sick,
I can't put any distance between us;
you're clever and intuitive,
anticipating every turn and twist I make;
besides, I seem to be held back by something:
call it weights round my ankles;
call it love.

Even when I believe I've escaped you,
you find a way of stopping me;
you say, you've told the hospital
I'm willing to take on five per cent
of the cancer cases; which means
that now everyone is chasing me.
I begin my rounds at the same time as I learn
I've got cancer myself;
I have to stop at the first toilet
because of my very first spell of nausea.

And that was just the beginning
of your hellish journey.
It's as if you're saying to me,
'You thought you were suffering!
You haven't lived yet, sunshine!'

3

Just as, thirty years ago,
you left me for a Surrey cricketer
because I was still tied up with my first wife,
and about a year later I rang your mother's home
wondering how you were – finding,
to my joy, he'd left you, broken the engagement,
having found letters from me in your handbag
leading him to think the coming child –
your lost but loved, adopted son –
was mine...

so, now, I think enough time
has passed, you'll have started to wonder
if I've forgotten you – I'll call
your mother's home and when you answer
I'll say, 'Oh God, Denise, how I've missed you!'
and maybe you'll come back.
We can still work things out.
I'm not that tied up;
I've not finished rowing with you,
and I can't believe you have with me.
Can't bear to think of you with this other guy.
I lift the phone.

4

Both of us in Hereford again, but separated;
you, teaching. We're doing okay:
you with a new man,
I with a new woman.
It all seems for the best.

Suddenly, though, I think of him
able to watch you, every morning,
putting on your suspender belt, drawing on
the black stockings and fastening them,
smoothing the skirt down;
and every night, watching you from the bed
taking them off; and occasionally, with a smile,
asking, 'Shall I leave them on?'...
Everyone knowing you're his now...
It's unbearable...

Waking, I realise you're not with anyone else,
you're simply dead;
and there's a moment of relief
until kicks in, as every morning, grief.

5

We're in Albania,
being hunted to the death.
You make me crouch down with you
by a window, and kiss,
so that if anyone spots us
they may think we're harmless lovers.
It doesn't work,
we're on the run again.
If we're caught, you say, pretend
we're trading in marmalade.
I protest we don't know anything about
trading marmalade.
A thug catches us.
You try to divert him
by opening your legs, your cunt
in crystal-sharp detail and close-up
between your white thighs and
fishnet stockings.
My God, this is very daring!
Even for a Channel Four art film
it would be daring.
Your ruse works. We make our escape,
still hunted.

6

You're sitting up in bed
at our friend Cath's,
looking plump in the face and glowing;
your hair's in an unfamiliar bouffant style,
rich and glossy. 'You look well!'
I exclaim happily.
You remove your wig
to be washed. 'Stupid man!' you say,
as you sometimes did.

7

Having got up, unable to sleep,
in the middle of the night,
I drink tea, smoke,
and make myself read through
these writings; change a few things.
It's painful, bringing back all that pain.

Are these visits of yours, these dream-meetings,
an illusion?

Later, you answer my question,
by snuggling at my side,
in your coat; I feel your solidity,
the warmth of your body; and you talk
animatedly, in your living accent
and your living earthy style.
They are real visits, you say.
I'm afraid to look at you,
as if you're Eurydice,
but at last I do, looking straight
into your face. It has aged a lot,
I assume through your suffering;
it's deeply lined;
but it doesn't matter, of course: it's you.

Coitus Interruptus

We've had our argument of thirty years
interrupted; and I've still not said everything.
Sitting across from me, at the kitchen table
messy with ashtrays and empty bottles, you'd say,
at five a.m. as I'd rise exhausted, 'That's right!
Walk out!' and I'd usually sit down again,
held by your fierce eyes, and our love of storms.
And if I slept for a couple of hours,
in the guest-room with the door locked,
I'd be rushed out of sleep by you bursting in
shouting, 'And another thing!...'

But now you've walked out on me;
and I haven't said everything.

3

Sunday Morning at Tesco's

Winter Dreams

(after Rilke)

Lord, it is time. The winter was too dark.
Remove Thy shadow from the sundial,
And still the gales that deflowered the park.

Tighten the laces of the balmy night
More and more swooningly; and cause to blossom
The opulent curves of light, the hips and bosom,
Until new life is aching with delight.

Who has no house now, will feel unencumbered;
Who's now alone, will make the warmth his friend;
Will walk late; sit at pavement cafes; and
The happiness, and even pain, remembered,
Will seem a passing girl's soft-brushing hand.

Listening to Bruckner

Bruckner unwinds, as grandly, as slowly,
As blessedly reluctant to let go,
As that summer day in Herefordshire,
'75 or '6 – two summers that were wholly
And endlessly summer, no wind to stir
The sunstruck trees, and every river low –

When Andrew, unable to face life,
Tired of the nightly nightmares,
Decided on a Bruckner Adagio,
The Eighth; politely asked his wife
If she minded. She said No,
And carried their small TV upstairs.

Laughing friends had gone, he'd driven his mistress home;
Empty bottles, glasses, wasp-bitten fruit
Brought in, he sat spilling more red wine
And ash on his crumpled, white, Edward Thomas suit,
Anticipating a continuation of the boredom;
Bruckner a whim, an LP out of line.

The long low room a shadowy island under
The sun still mystically in the sky,
He felt a slight enthusiasm spark
A need for symphony after symphony
Drenching him in the music's simple wonder;
His wife asleep, cottage and meadows dark,

I see him – his cigar's fade and glow,
A wine glass moving to his lips; his swift
Lurch to turn over, or replace the First
With the Seventh, the Ninth, the Fourth; his thirst
Boundless for the sweet strings, then the lift
To mountain thunder. Twenty-five years ago.

Dawn took him by surprise. He went to bed.
And woke – in the wide bed I shared with them
When drunk sometimes – to his amazement, fresh;
No nightmares jangling in his clear head.
He thought death must be like that – safe from harm,
An essence, with no need of waking flesh.

I don't know what he played while he was waiting
For sleep to take him, two years later in
The Oxford flat, his second wife away;
But think of Urdimarsh, the grey dawn hesitating
Then turning to another burning day,
And the Adagio waiting to begin.

Imagining Russia

We'll start with the hinterland. Dark Russia
Of glaring muzhiks, dirty as the pigs and chickens.
Beatroot and sour milk – if we stay overnight I swear
I'll top myself. You'll be saying, "Donald Garoldovich has
                                            died."
The cretinous priest has got a girl in trouble.
You say, "It's wonderful!" but I know you're lying.

We stay the night. The guy with the truck was lying.
But as we look out at silent Mother Russia,
With her story that makes our Anglo-Irish Troubles
Seem like a barnyard fracas between chickens,
Taking in moon and birches, the brown muck dyed
Grey, with exquisite streaks of white, we swear

We'll never leave. We leave. Our driver swears
As his truck sputters. Three days on, we're lying
Where one stroke of a pen meant thousands died.
Then Stalin watched a Western. In his Russia
Heads jerked around in constant fear, like chickens'.
You died if you were brave, or if you gave no trouble.

I browse my slovár. "There's no word for 'trouble',
It's too mild... Górye is grief... They swear
Like us, 'Go fuck your mother!'"... Gnawing chicken
And smoking between bites on the love-train; then lying,
Bunk over bunk, speeding at night between Russia's
Two capitals. "I still call it Leningrad... 'He's dead!

He's dead!' Pasternak sobbed as Zhivago died
In his novel. Dying himself, Boris was troubled
That his mistress Olga – his Lara, his Russia –
Would see him without teeth. Made his wife swear
Not to admit her. 'He won't see you!' his wife said, lying
Truthfully..." I think of home, our four chickens

Pecking in the garden. You're silent. I'm too chicken
To ask what you're thinking. I wept when Pushkin died
In Troyat's biography. I see the poet lying
Begging his friends to forgive him all this trouble.
"I'll show you the sphinxes by the Neva. I swear
Tomorrow, dushá, you'll understand Russia."

Still you are silent, breathing gently. I swear
A woman's heart is more complex than Russia.
If that moon said she understood it, she'd be lying.

Jeekes House

The Tudor guest-house we stumbled into
In Rye, shaking off the snow of a bitter day,
Had been restored and lived in by a poet
We found. Conrad Aitken. I browsed, before a fire,
Sherry warming us, his 'Selected Letters' from a shelf –
Letters to odd wives and mistresses; jokes about
His botched suicide; his love for the house.

It should have been filled with his ghost,
And ghosts of deeply troubled women;
Ghosts in his mind from those
Parents who gave him lessons in suicide
He didn't learn well: and murder too:
His father killed his wife and then himself.
How the child must have felt he'd let him down.
But no, the house was calm, our four-poster attuned
To love; Mozart played in the breakfast-room;
The guest-book was filled with 'lovely', 'peaceful'.

As if his poetry used up his pain,
As if he'd lived it all – even death – before he died;
And went out, turned the key, and so was gone,
Completely gone, leaving no pain behind,
But just 'Selected Letters' on a shelf,
Leaving a guest-book empty and unsullied.

Court of Enquiry, Madras, 1904

Questions this court is seeking answers for:
Was the deceased Adela Nicolson Cory,
A general's widow, and a poetess
Called Laurence Hope – the name they know her by
In English parlours?   Did she choose to die
By her own hand in a most dreadful fashion,
Ingesting mercury, and if so, why?
Why did a wellbred girl from Gloucestershire,
Choosing to wed a colonel twice her years,
Go native in her language, manners, dress
And culture – even sati, since she appears
To have evaded friends, dying by stealth
Before the flowers had withered on his tomb?

There are no questions we shall disallow.
Why does her last work, on her escritoire,
With crisp instructions for her publisher,
Still burn with that intense erotic passion,
Softened by India and a male nom de plume?
I find at random 'Chalice of Pleasure'…'Shrine
Of Mysterious Power'…What could these mean
To a wife and mother, near her change of life?
– Or this, a girl's breasts hacked off by the knife
Of her dishonoured lord ..? The dedication
To Nicolson, 'Small joy was I to thee…'
Shows sad, respectful love – field-rations,
None of her Jasmin-scented ecstasy.
Was he as cool at home as under fire?
Or gnawed by sorrow, till it broke his health?

We must, before the summer chokes Madras,
See with this woman's thoughtful, sombre eyes,
Put on her sari, her embroidered shoes.
Was all her verse invention or translation?
Or was there unendurable remorse
She had to numb with savage poison? Whose
Were the pale hands beside the Shalimar
She loved?   For whom did she so madly ride

Through ice, before dawn, as the flame inside
Her turned the cold, far peaks to paradise?
And does she now at last know happiness,
Some piercing love, joy throbbing like a star?
Was death the rapturous love-bite without bruise?
Where is she now? Where is she now?

Note: The poet 'Laurence Hope' committed suicide
in October 1904, aged 39, two months after the death
of her 62-year-old husband, General Nicolson.

Sunday Morning at Tesco's

(rondeau redoublé)

We won't exactly starve!... Merlot... Gruyère?...
My drifty, not unpleasant ritual.
In the old world, where sinners bent in prayer,
The Burning Bush, and so on, bored us all.

These lithe Doc Martened girls can booze and brawl;
The earringed lads can cook a meal with flare;
None can sing 'Love Divine', or quote St.Paul.
We didn't starve exactly, though Gruyère

Was unknown foreign muck, and drink a snare.
Our lives enclosed by dark carns, a knackt bal,
Men had their Institute; wives permed their hair;
Saturday's bus brought the sweet ritual –

Say, Bogart, with a bullet-bra'd, wide-hipped moll.
These trousered, sneakered couples merge and share,
Woman was Psyche, moon, and night, and soul,
In the old world. Sin – huddling for the prayer –

Was sliding a skirt back, resting my hand where
The clasp of a suspender would enthrall;
Like Moses, I'd avoid the holy lair,
Her burning bush. Its mystery awed us all.

Freed-up, we're at the Tesco Value stall,
Dull eyes not even knowing what's not there;
Gone now, the burning bush, the irrational;
God, like the girdle, slimmed to light shapewear.
But we don't starve exactly.

knackt bal – ruined mine (Cornish)

Poetry Reading

Almost too diffident to choose,
His hand skims his slim paperbacks;
Matronly arses in tight slacks
And grey men trying to look sage,
A dozen scattered round the hall,
Sit patient as the poet um's
From page to page before he comes
To something low-keyed, trivial,
He might, um, read. His voice, a moth's

Slow stuttering flight. My brain grows numb.
This is the English idiom:
Reserved free verse, laconic, slight.
Two hours of this and I can't smoke.
I sip the complimentary plonk.
My eyes stray to the double-doors;
If only Anna's 'drunks and whores'
Frequenting Petersburg's 'Stray Dogs',
Herself among them, skirt worn tight,
Would burst in with their fug of smoke,
And show him what poetry's about!

I think of Alexander Blok,
'The tragic tenor of his age',
His eyes like an electric shock;
Of Osip Mandelstam, that verse
Which sent the Kremlin mountaineer
Into a paroxysm of rage
And him to labour camps and death
From typhus near Vladivostok.

I think of how his widow knew
Each line of his entire work
By heart; though scarcely dared to sleep
For fear she might forget a line.
Of course it helped her that he wrote
In metre, the device by which
A poem can memorise itself.
For poems without form we keep
Having to reach up to the shelf.

His voice still flutters like a moth.
I could have stayed at home to wank.
I fix my gaze upon the wall
Of the bleak assembly hall,
Seeing, in well-typed Roman, verse –
Or so it looks; it can't be worse
Than his; I blink to clear my eyes…
No, it's 'In the event of fire.'
That's droll… We have his poetry,
There's no fire that it can't control.

Imagine – dear God! – memorising
This poet's work! There's just one line
Of his I love, and know by heart;
Almost sublime, and as surprising
As, through black clouds, a harvest moon:
'And now, um, now… perhaps… to end…'
Not yet. Not yet. Stalin, old friend,
Send in your thugs. An instant burst.
Then bury him in some silent wood.

Stray Dogs: a cabaret in pre-Revolutionary Petersburg
noted for poetry and dissipation.

Re-making 'Brief Encounter'

We hear one strangled gasp, as Laura melts
In Alec's arms; there's just one thrust, unseen,
The camera on her eyes, or stocking-welts,
Before his friend's shock entry ends the scene.
Then we see Fred as, gratefully completing
'Huge cloudy symbols of a high romance',
He flashbacks to that morning's anguished, fleeting
Lech in a Gents, a chap's hand in his pants.
Then, as the last Rach swells, their doorbell rings:
It's Alec, mad with love. The affair's revealed.
They talk it through till dawn. Next Thursday brings
A tender, lustful threesome. All is healed.
Alec will stay in England. Laura tingles;
And Fred's released from sordid, dangerous singles.

Thrill of Flying

(for Victoria)

She loves to fly – to Rome, Tashkent, or Riga –
So great her urge to drink all beauty in;
If it had landing-strips, she'd fly to Vega,
With a light suncream on her English skin.
That star, the purest blue in all creation,
Shines so, I know astronomers who swear
She did indeed go, in some incarnation,
And left the brightness of her presence there.
And yet at home she's equally
At home, and never happier than when
She's making marmalade or poetry;
Sadness runs shadowing her joyous laughter,
As when she leads to roost her 'girls', three hens,
Who somehow sense it's love they hurry after.

Tolstoy's Birthday

(Yasnaya Polyana, 9th September 2002)

Even the sky
has a sense of occasion;
yesterday's grey, rainy autumn
turning again to late summer;
a soft blue radiance
touching the high trees and
the crackly fallen leaves with gold.

A vivacity of teenagers
on a morning off school
with their teachers
listens respectfully to ageing authors
singing his praises through a hand-mike.
Every girl wears the bright lipstick
he'd have disapproved of
while burning for that sinful flesh.

Then, to the grave without a stone,
just a green mound,
where Lev's brother told him, in boyhood,
a green stick was planted;
it held, for anyone who found it,
the secret of happiness.

I have found the green stick.
Invited into a group photo
by an excited teenager,
in the close, arms-round-each-other huddle,
I feel her soft, sweet, growing breast
pressed unselfconsciously
against me.

Tommy Beer

Tommy Beer
was king of Southgate Street, Redruth,
back in the 50's: stalking up and down
the poor terraces, no known ties,
no address I knew of, an air
of endless leisure; laconic, witty,
could put on a posh voice; working-class spiv,
swarthy, dirty, curiously raffish too
with unwashed brylcreamed hair, sometimes
a slightly grubby red
cravate; a natural aristocrat
absurdly ignored by Debrett's.

Keen supporter of the Reds,
rugby or cricket. I recall him,
after a game at Penzance,
borrowing a guard's cap on the train home,
opening carriage-door after carriage-door and announcing,
in his most Etonian accent,
'We're now approaching Camborne; you can tell that
from the black clouds ahead.' Upcountry faces gaping
as he closed the door on them.
I admired him, yet never wanted to get close.

I see him sometimes now, on Saturday afternoons
at the Redruth Recre.: frail, lurching,
in a filthy mac, Dorian Gray's his face,
but somehow the same old Tommy Beer;
and I think, in my camel overcoat, walking slowly
to the same outdoor urinal:
'I too am still here, still here.'

The Other Country

At twelve, Donald Craze and I
played timeless Test-matches
in Mr Caddy's field behind 'Beverly'
all the hot summer holidays;
England against South Africa, in line
with real Tests on flatter fields elsewhere.

We were tireless: each of us captain,
batsmen, bowlers, keeper, fielders, umpires,
and kept meticulous scorecards.
I chose South Africa, from my Dad's
anti-imperial bias; though Donald Craze
had all the glamour,
Edrich and Compton in their golden summer.

Ours was a series of the unexpected.
An Athol Rowan offspin landing on
a cowpat could bowl out Len Hutton
with a vast legbreak. One day I
was Dudley Nourse, my hero, when
Mum appeared and called me to come in.
It was dusking, but she wasn't offering me
the light; it was an order.

I snarled 'Fuck!' not knowing
what it meant. Bewildered, I found myself
in bed within minutes; the only time
I was ever punished. I lay there
wondering why a word had so upset her,
vaguely aware I was in some other country,
awesome, non-cricketplaying.
Soon Dad came home from work
and said I could get up,

and took me in his work's van
to visit our relatives in Carnkie.
It was like, ten years later, just before his death,
he told me to jump in the car when I'd got
a postcard saying I'd won a First.
I think, that first time too, he was proud of me –
not Mummy's boy any more,
or not so much; was in that other country
he lived in secretly and with some shame.

Next morning Nourse reached fifty with a hit
that landed in a crusty pat and stayed
while I ran six between stumps and jacket.

Penalty

I'm still an active sportsman in my dreams,
but only at the highest level.
At my age you have to husband your energy.
I've played rugby for England
and the occasional cricket Test.
The dream-selectors know the value of experience.

They seem mercifully to forget that in every
international I let the team down
because my legs seem to be stuck in treacle;
their sage august heads still nod vigorously
when they come to my name.

Five years ago I captained England at soccer.
At half time the scores were level.
When we were awarded a penalty
everyone knew I would take it – even David
Beckham withdrew to the touchline. I placed
the ball on the spot, withdrew a few paces; poised
to hit it. Then froze completely.

One minute became five; became ten.
My players stood patiently. I just couldn't run up.
It was like a writer's block, which I know about,
It was like the block that blocked Blok
when the Revolution turned ugly, or
when he was in love with two women called Love,
Liubov'. I know about that too.
The light was fading. Ten minutes became twenty, thirty.
All the players and officials walked off the field.

It was really dark now.
I knew I had to hit the great white dome of St. Sophia
looming behind the goal. I didn't think I could do it.
A full moon rose over the Bosphorus.

Biographical note

D.M. Thomas was born in Redruth, Cornwall, in 1935. After attending Grammar Schools in Redruth and Melbourne, Australia, he was awarded a First in English at New College, Oxford. For many years he was a teacher and lecturer, while writing and publishing poetry. In 1979 he became a full-time writer. He has published seven collections of verse, including *The Puberty Tree* (1992); thirteen novels, including the modern classic *The White Hotel* (1981), translated into twenty seven languages; translations of Russian poetry, a biography, a memoir and a stage play, *Hell Fire Corner*. He has won a Cholmondeley Prize for poetry, the Los Angeles Times fiction prize, and the Orwell Prize for his biography of Solzhenitsyn. He has a daughter and two sons, and lives in Truro with his third wife, Victoria Field.

For further information and a bibliography please consult
www.dmthomasonline.com